Can you imagine...?

Can you imagine....?

a Counting book

Text and Graphics
by Beau Gardner

Dodd, Mead & Company, New York

1 one

1 whale wearing a veil?

2 two

2 ducks driving trucks?

3 three

3 giraffes
taking photographs?

4 four

4 armadillos
sleeping on pillows?

5 five

5 bears climbing stairs?

6 six

6 goats trying on coats?

7 seven

7 raccoons carrying balloons

8 eight

8 snakes serving cakes?

10 ten

10 otters
playing on teeter-totters?

11 eleven

11 squirrels dressed in pearls?

12 twelve

12 swans twirling batons?

1	one
2	two
3	three
4	four
5	five
6	six

7	seven
8	eight
9	nine
10	ten
11	eleven
12	twelve

To my
daughters,
nephews and
nieces:

Stacey
Mari
Keri
Kami
Steffani
John
Mark
Michael
Matt
Jeremy
Susanne
Glenn
Brian
Joey
Krissy
Tommy
Beau
Brandon
Jay
David

With special
thanks to:

Anne Simon
Margaret Pascocello
Randi Steinbach
Betty Schwartz

Published by Dodd, Mead & Company, Inc.,
71 Fifth Avenue, New York, NY 10003
Printed in Hong Kong by
South China Printing Company
1 2 3 4 5 6 7 8 9 10

Library of Congress Cataloging-in-Publication Data

Gardner, Beau.
Can you imagine— ?

Summary: Rhyming text introduces
animals and numbers
from one whale wearing a veil
to twelve swans twirling batons.
1. Counting—Juvenile literature.
[1. Counting. 2. Animals—Fiction]
I. Title.
QA113.G37   1987
513′.2   87-13520
ISBN 0-396-09001-X